BETRAYAL CAN SHAKE THE VERY FOUNDATION OF YOUR WORLD.

It leaves you questioning everything—your worth, your choices, and even your future. But let me tell you this: you are not broken, and you are not alone. Healing is possible, and this 7-day journey is here to help you take the first steps toward reclaiming your peace, confidence, and strength. Each day, you will be guided through powerful reflections, scripture-based encouragement, and challenges designed to help you move forward—not just surviving, but thriving. This is your time to heal, to rise, and to walk boldly into the future God has for you.

Notes

HOW TO USE THIS BOOK

Healing is not a one-time event; it's a process. This book is designed to guide you through the first steps of your journey, but your growth and healing will continue beyond these seven days. Each section includes an inspirational message, scripture, reflection, and challenge to help you process your emotions and take steps toward restoration.

To get the most out of this challenge, consider purchasing a journal or notebook to complete the daily reflections and challenges. Writing down your thoughts will help you track your progress, release emotions, and see how far you've come. Be patient with yourself and embrace this journey one day at a time.

ACKNOWLEDING THE PAIN

WHAT HAPPENED TO YOU WAS NOT YOUR FAULT. LET'S GET THAT STRAIGHT.

You didn't cause it, and you don't deserve to carry the weight of someone else's choices. Pain is inevitable, but staying in it is optional. Acknowledge the pain, but don't let it define you.

PSALM 34:18
"THE LORD IS CLOSE TO THE BROKENHEARTED AND SAVES THOSE WHO ARE CRUSHED IN SPIRIT."

REFLECTION

Betrayal cuts deep, and it's okay to feel the pain. Acknowledge your emotions without guilt.

CHALLENGE

Write down your emotions honestly in a journal. Pour out your heart in prayer and ask God to meet you in your brokenness.

RELEASING THE BURDEN

YOU DON'T HAVE TO CARRY THIS ALONE.

The burden of betrayal is heavy, and it's time to put it down. It's not a sign of weakness to let go—it's a sign of strength. Real strength comes from surrendering what you can't control and trusting God to handle the rest.

MATTHEW 11:28 "COME TO ME, ALL YOU WHO ARE WEARY AND BURDENED, AND I WILL GIVE YOU REST."

REFLECTION

Carrying the weight of betrayal alone will exhaust you. Surrender your pain to God.

CHALLENGE

Take 10 minutes to meditate on this verse. Visualize handing your pain over to God. Write a letter expressing your emotions but do not send it.

GUARDING YOUR HEART

YOU ARE WORTH PROTECTING.

Your heart, your peace, your joy—none of these should be up for grabs. Set the boundaries you need, and don't apologize for them. Healing isn't about pleasing others; it's about taking care of yourself first.

PROVERBS 4:23 "ABOVE ALL ELSE, GUARD YOUR HEART, FOR EVERYTHING YOU DO FLOWS FROM IT."

REFLECTION

Your heart is precious. Protect it from bitterness and resentment as you heal.

CHALLENGE

List three healthy boundaries that will protect your heart during this process and commit to enforcing them.

CHOOSING FORGIVENESS

FORGIVENESS ISN'T ABOUT THEM—IT'S ABOUT YOU.

It doesn't mean what happened was okay, and it doesn't mean you have to forget. It means you are choosing to free yourself from the chains of resentment. You deserve peace more than they deserve your anger.

COLOSSIANS 3:13
"BEAR WITH EACH OTHER AND FORGIVE ONE ANOTHER IF ANY OF YOU HAS A GRIEVANCE AGAINST SOMEONE. FORGIVE AS THE LORD FORGAVE YOU."

REFLECTION

Forgiveness is for your healing, not theirs. It doesn't excuse the offense, but it frees you from its hold.

CHALLENGE

Write down any lingering anger or unforgiveness and pray over it. Ask God to help you take steps toward releasing it.

REBUILDING CONFIDENCE

BETRAYAL DOESNT DEFINE YOU

You are not broken, unworthy, or less-than because of someone else's actions. You are strong, capable, and worthy of love and respect. Don't let this experience steal your confidence—take it back.

PSALM 139:14
"I PRAISE YOU BECAUSE I AM FEARFULLY AND WONDERFULLY MADE; YOUR WORKS ARE WONDERFUL, I KNOW THAT FULL WELL."

REFLECTION

Betrayal can make you question your worth, but your value comes from God, not others.

CHALLENGE

Write five affirmations about yourself and say them aloud daily. Reflect on God's view of you.

EMBRACING PEACE

PEACE IS YOUR BIRTHRIGHT, NOT A PRIVILEGE.

It's not something you have to earn; it's something you are meant to have. Chaos may have knocked on your door, but you don't have to let it move in. Claim your peace and protect it fiercely.

JOHN 14:27
"PEACE I LEAVE WITH YOU; MY PEACE I GIVE YOU. I DO NOT GIVE TO YOU AS THE WORLD GIVES. DO NOT LET YOUR HEARTS BE TROUBLED AND DO NOT BE AFRAID."

REFLECTION

Healing brings peace. Trust that God is restoring you.

CHALLENGE

Set aside 15 minutes for quiet time today. Breathe deeply, pray, and meditate on God's peace.

STEPPING INTO RENEWAL

THIS IS NOT THE END OF YOUR STORY.

What was meant to break you will become the foundation for your greatest comeback. You are walking into something new, something better. Let go of the past, step boldly into your future, and never look back.

ISAIAH 43:19
"SEE, I AM DOING A NEW THING! NOW IT SPRINGS UP; DO YOU NOT PERCEIVE IT? I AM MAKING A WAY IN THE WILDERNESS AND STREAMS IN THE WASTELAND."

REFLECTION

You are not defined by your past. God has a new path for you.

CHALLENGE

Write down one step you will take toward your renewed future. Pray for strength and direction.

Notes

REMEMBER

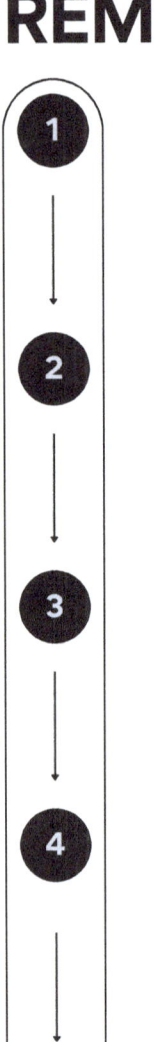

WORTH

Your worth is not determined by someone else's actions. You are valuable, loved, and deserving of respect.

HEALING

Healing takes time. Give yourself grace, and don't rush the process.

CHOICE

You have the power to choose. Whether you stay or leave, the decision should be based on what brings you peace and aligns with God's will.

REBUILD

Reconciliation is a two-way street. If your spouse is unwilling to rebuild trust with accountability and true repentance, you cannot force healing in the relationship.

WELL-BEING

Prepare for the next steps. Seek wise counsel, pray for clarity, and take practical steps to secure your emotional, spiritual, and financial well-being.

Notes